the
REALLY
really
BUSY PERSON'S
book on
PARENTING

To the friends and supporters of Care for the Family – you are changing lives – Thank You!

the REALLY *really* BUSY PERSON'S *book on* PARENTING

Rob Parsons & Katharine Hill

Muddy Pearl

First published in 2015 by
Muddy Pearl, Edinburgh, Scotland.

www.muddypearl.com
books@muddypearl.com

© Care for the Family

Cartoons © David McNeill 2015

Rob Parsons and Katharine Hill have asserted their right under the
Copyright, Designs and Patents Act, 1988 to be identified as the
authors of this work.

British Library Cataloguing in Publication Data.
A catalogue record for this book is available from the British Library

ISBN 978-1-910012-28-4

Typeset and designed by RevoCreative. www.revocreative.co.uk

Printed and bound in Great Britain by Bell and Bain Ltd, Glasgow

ACKNOWLEDGMENTS

Thanks to the whole team at Care for the Family and especially our brilliant Senior Editor, Sheron Rice. As always, Stephanie and Richard of Muddy Pearl have been amazing – we love working with you guys! And a very big thank you to David McNeill – we couldn't have done it without you!

We were recently chatting to a good friend over a cup of coffee about the ups and downs of family life. We looked back over the good times and the moments we would rather forget – sleepless nights too numerous to mention, bedtime stories, giggles in the dark, milk teeth, croup, dressing up, shoe laces, school runs, chickenpox, birthday parties, the teenage years (and more sleepless nights!) shopping trips, school discos, exams, broken hearts, gap year adventures, college … and, before we know it, our children are adults and making their own way in the world.

We began talking about the past twenty-five years at Care for the Family (the charity that Rob founded and of which Katharine is the UK Director) and the million people we have spoken to in live events across the world. And as we talked about the parenting books we have written, the advice we have given (and received!), and the brilliant parenting quotes we have heard over the years, our friend asked us what our favourite bits were. That conversation got us thinking. We teamed up with brilliant cartoonist and illustrator David McNeill, and gathered together our 'favourite bits' into this little book. There are some that made us laugh and some that made us cry, but we think all of them give wisdom, encouragement and hope to mums and dads in the incredible task that is parenting.

*So put the coffee on, enjoy the honesty of some of the parents who have shared their ideas with us, and allow yourself a smile at David's wonderful cartoons. But most of all, we want you to know for certain that whatever you are going through at this moment – a brand new baby who cries all night, a toddler who only will eat jammy dodgers or a teenager who decides he definitely hates you – you are not alone. When we grasp that wonderful truth we are set free to believe what, in our hearts, we knew all along: there is no one way to be a **perfect** parent but there are a hundred ways to be a **great** parent!*

No authors deserve to have as much fun putting a book together as we have. We really hope you enjoy it!

Rob and Katharine

THE REALLY REALLY BUSY PERSON'S...

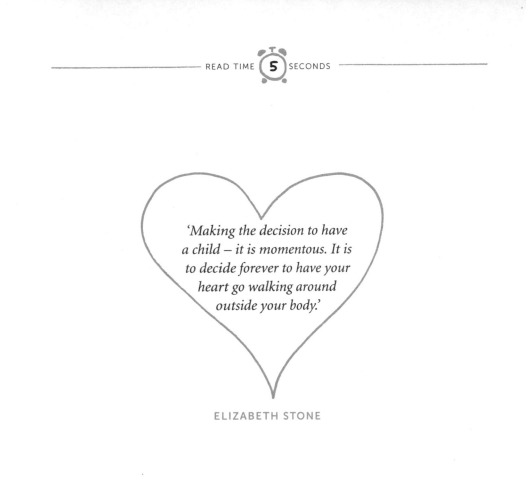

'*Making the decision to have a child – it is momentous. It is to decide forever to have your heart go walking around outside your body.*'

ELIZABETH STONE

When it comes to their own children, there are no 'experts' – just people trying to get their own families through as best they can.

> *I think a good parent isn't one who makes dinner or helps you with homework because I can do that myself, but a person who is always there for you no matter what and will always love and accept you for who you are.*

13-YEAR-OLD GIRL

I naïvely assumed that the struggle to conceive, eight-and-a-half months of nausea followed by a night of hard labour meant that the difficult bit was over, and I looked forward to life as a mummy with a mixture of excitement and anticipation. I had somehow overlooked the fact that this was just the beginning. The journey of parenthood had really only just begun.

In giving our children boundaries appropriate for their age, we are giving them a gift: we are building in them a deep sense of security that will last a lifetime.

Two-year-olds are not fooled by designs like a clown with a mashed potato face, a sausage nose, pea eyes, a carrot smile and broccoli hair.

THEY KNOW WHAT BROCCOLI IS.

Build up all the respect you can when they are small ...

YOU'RE GOING TO NEED IT.

I know it's difficult when your toddler is stamping and kicking in the supermarket because she wants a bag of sweets. She may be threatening to embarrass you by throwing cartons of yoghurt over the other shoppers unless she gets her way. But if you do choose to fight that battle, then even if a dozen customers go home covered from head to foot in 'Müller Light', make sure you win it. The reason is clear: although it's hard at the time, it doesn't come near, not anywhere near, having a 14-year-old girl looking you in the eye and saying 'No'.

A slower day is not coming. If you have anything that matters to you, try to give some time to it **today**.

SOMETIMES WE HAVE
TO LOVE OUR KIDS
WHEN WE DON'T 'LIKE'
THEM VERY MUCH.

One of our goals as parents is to equip our
children to make good choices in a world
where choices are unlimited.

With regard to our children and exams, remember that the best 'A star' is emotional health. I think of a girl desperate to please her parents and teachers. She got nine 'A stars' and one 'A' – and almost had a breakdown over dropping that one star. And I remember the boy who considered hacking into his school's computer system to raise his maths grade by a couple of points. The role of a parent with a child who puts themselves under pressure like this is not to push them even harder, but to bring a little perspective.

You're not the only mother who, when your second baby arrives, abandons all those great ideals you had with the first.

I feel pretty confident as an adult and I think
one reason for this is that the first man in
my life – my dad – made me feel special.

I wish someone had told me that glowing mother love is not automatically delivered with the baby and that you don't feel like the mum on the baby food advert who has time to roll around on a white bed-cover in her size eight jeans.

I was at the airport waiting for my flight when I became aware of a commotion at the table next to me. Two lively blond-haired boys were wrestling on the bench, knocking table napkins, paper cups and teaspoons to the floor. A young mum desperately tried to referee, whilst Granny sat nearby looking on disapprovingly.

A few minutes later we boarded the plane. At the eleventh hour, two familiar blond heads came bobbing down the aisle. The passengers seated on either side ducked for cover as the boys' rucksacks bumped against them. Finally, the plane took off. And so did the boys.

Granny was having none of it. She told the boys off and then turned on her daughter-in-law to tell her where she was going wrong in her parenting. My heart went out to this young mum, trying her best. These boys were simply being boys, but the confines of the plane made it seem like they were misbehaving.

We landed and as people began to get off the plane I hung back then went up to her and said, 'You're doing a great job.' She practically hugged me.

There are no easy answers for a mum in that situation, but just once in a while we all need someone to hang back and say to us, 'Well done. Great job!'

Children need to know that their parents sometimes get it wrong. I once heard a father boast, 'I have never, nor would I ever, apologise to my son.'

You can fear a man like that, but it's hard to respect him and even harder to have a deep relationship with him.

LABEL THE ACTION,
NEVER THE CHILD.

Rather than commenting on our children –
'You are so selfish/unkind/naughty ...' – we
would do well to describe their behaviour.
So instead of, 'You were so unkind to leave
Lottie out of your game', we might say,
'That was an unkind thing to do when you
wouldn't let Lottie join in your game.' In
describing their behaviour, it leaves open
the possibility of change.

Don't be too upset when your kids don't want the meal you made. I know it doesn't help when your son comes home and says, 'Tom's mum did us egg on toast'. You say, 'But you don't like eggs!', and he replies, 'I do when Tom's mum makes them.' It is hurtful, but it's not personal.

CATCH YOUR KIDS DOING SOMETHING RIGHT.

There are ten words that as a parent you should commit to memory. In fact, get them inscribed onto your bedroom ceiling so you see them on waking and they burn into your soul at night:

'DON'T TAKE ALL THE CREDIT; DON'T TAKE ALL THE BLAME.'

*We had a little game we would play with
the children at meal times that helped us
communicate together. It was called High-Low
and we would simply ask each other what our
'High' and then our 'Low' of the day or the week
was. Nine times out of ten the children wouldn't
co-operate, but just occasionally we would hear
of a falling out in the playground or a goal
scored in a football match that we wouldn't have
known about otherwise. Take the time to ask your
children about their day. You may be surprised
what you discover!*

WHEN THE EAR NEVER
HEARS PRAISE, THE
HEART LOSES THE WILL
TO TRY.

You're not the only mother who stays up all night making a dozen flapjacks for the school fair cake stall and then doesn't produce them on seeing that Danielle Thomas' mother has made a novelty cake in the shape of a tree-house complete with squirrel. You go straight home and eat all the flapjacks.

PARENT WITH
ELASTIC

As parents, we're hard-wired to protect our children. It's as if we want to keep them on the end of a tight piece of string and to make sure they stay safe and are equipped for every eventuality. But a wise friend once said to me, 'Don't use string, use elastic.' If we use string from the beginning, then as they seek their independence, that string will go taut and eventually snap. But if we use elastic, it will gradually stretch when we give them more responsibility as they grow up.

KEEP A FAMILY QUOTE BOOK – FUNNY, EMBARRASSING, PROFOUND.

There has to come a point where, no matter how much paint the five-year-old has tipped over the new carpet or how deep the hurt the teenager has caused, it can be dealt with and forgotten. None of us can survive if the past is thrown at us every time we make a new mistake.

I am a mother. I am not a perfect mother – I
learnt a long time ago that 'perfect' is too
great a burden to carry.

As a new parent I enjoyed going to our local parent and toddler group. One morning we were all sitting round with our babies on the mats on the floor, when suddenly one little boy spotted a red engine on the far side of the room and set off to get it. The rest of us were amazed – our babies could barely lift their heads, let alone crawl. This baby was then enveloped with hugs by his mother and smothered with praise from everyone else around. He looked a little shocked, not quite sure what he had done to be at the centre of all this attention. But that day, this young boy had learnt a lesson for life: people like us when we achieve and do well. When we get older we find that the world hasn't changed very much.

As parents we have the opportunity to give our children a different message. Whether or not they come top in the spelling test, win prizes at school, get into the sports team, or are chosen for the school play, we can show them that our love for them isn't based on what they achieve, but on who they are. The most precious gift we can give to our children is to let them know that they are loved ... anyway.

There is only one thing more annoying than seeing wonderful parents who have children who test them to the core. It is meeting parents who have broken every rule in the book, but whose children turn out beautifully.

Even in a technological age, children love
getting things through the post – letters,
postcards, little surprises.

DON'T READ YOUR CHILD'S SCHOOL REPORTS AS THOUGH THEY ARE A PROPHECY OF THEIR FUTURE LIVES.

I know your child's school reports might be a little depressing. I used to believe my maths teacher loved me because she put kisses by my sums. But remember that although reports are important, there's lots they don't measure – emotional intelligence, savvy and the ability some kids have to really make things happen. Some children develop a little later and, anyway, when they discover something they really want to do in life, then everything changes.

WHEN THEY WERE
VERY YOUNG YOU
USED TO TICKLE THEM.
DON'T EVER STOP.

DON'T STRIVE FOR PERFECTION. LIFE'S HARD ENOUGH WITHOUT TRYING TO WIN A PARENTING OSCAR.

Enforcing the rules is not just a matter of discipline; it is a matter of security. There is no faster way to breed insecurity in a child than for them to believe there are no boundaries – and that even if there are, nobody cares if they are crossed.

In our experience few parents want to be known as 'disciplinarians', but they do want to have a measure of control over their children. With this in mind, it's good to get a few easy 'wins' in the bag while they are very young. We want to convey the lesson that when Mum and Dad say something, they mean it. One mum said, 'I would actually look for situations when I could teach the link between bad behaviour and consequences. Sometimes I would say to my three-year-old, 'If you do that again, we're not going to the park!' I knew she'd do it again – and that was fine because I didn't want to go to the park anyway!

Ah, if it were only possible to stay so far in front when they are teenagers.

I am not 'just' a mother. I am a woman with gifts, hopes and desires that are unconnected to my two kids. But, without doubt, it is in the realm of motherhood that you will find my greatest laughter and my deepest sorrow; it is there you will discover my greatest pride and haunting fears.

When it comes to discipline,
'Shoulder to shoulder' is not
a bad mantra for couples
parenting together.

IF YOU WANT TO GET A
CHILD WHO'S ALMOST
ASLEEP FULLY AWAKE, TRY
SKIPPING TWO PAGES OF
A BEDTIME STORY.

It's tough being a single parent. There's nobody to say, 'Don't be daft' or 'Let the baby cry for a while' or 'You're doing a great job.' I so often have the sense that I really am on my own. Even ordinary things can seem like mountains to climb. I'm scared of getting 'flu because somebody has to care for my kids. The other day I had to go into hospital for a minor operation, but first I had to get somebody to have my two children for a couple of days. You'd think it would be easy, but sometimes it seems impossible.

I was a disappointment to my father He wanted a son. He never hugged me, praised me, or told me he loved me. I realised he was a product of his generation and I have forgiven him but my self-esteem is very low. I am often depressed, I am riddled with guilt

... *I am eighty-five years old.*

Start a memory box with each of your kids.
Fill it with little treasures and mementoes.
Every so often, get it out and look through
it together.

Sometimes we are so busy giving our kids
what we didn't have, that we don't have time
to give them what we did have.

When they are grown, your children will
forget the expensive presents you bought
them: the plasma TV, the bike with 50 gears
– all will be forgotten. They'll remember the
night when they were nine and you slept
in the garden in a tent with them and at
midnight an owl hooted and you were both
so scared you came back into the house.

A head teacher used to send a letter home to the kids' parents on the first day of school:

Dear Parent,

If you promise not to believe all that your child tells you goes on at school,
I promise not to believe all that they tell me goes on at home.

(Most parents were prepared to sign the deal in blood.)

It's not always possible, but try to give your children your time when they are small. When they're teenagers they'll say, 'Great idea, Dad. But would you mind if we did it later?'

COMPARISON IS NOT A GOOD TOOL TO KEEP IN THE TOOLBOX OF PARENTING.

It's so easy to look sideways and feel that everybody else is doing a much better job than you, and then to feel bad. I spend half my life hoping my kids won't give the game away about what I'm really like as a mother, but actually I'm giving it my best shot and my kids are fine.

THERE ARE TWO
THINGS WE SHOULD
GIVE OUR CHILDREN:
ONE IS ROOTS AND
THE OTHER IS WINGS.

One dad said:

When I'm gone and my children talk about me, I would love them to say that I taught them great things, to look at the world with large eyes, to reach their potential and to care for others. But I would wonder if I had missed it if they didn't add, 'But what we remember too is that he was fun to be with'.

So often when I ask adults to tell me what made their family life sweet they begin the sentence with the words 'We always ...': 'We always did ... on a Saturday morning', 'We always did ... at Christmas.'

Family traditions are important. One expert said that they give a child a sense of connectedness. They say to the child, 'You belong here. This is your family. This is the way our family does things. These are your roots.'

The annoying thing about being a parent is just about the time you get the hang of it – you're redundant!

ASK YOUR KIDS FOR THEIR OPINIONS ON THINGS – TRIVIAL AND SERIOUS. IT'S PART OF THEIR GROWING UP PROCESS.

I DON'T NEED TO USE
GOOGLE BECAUSE MY
TEENAGER KNOWS
EVERYTHING.

Has an issue with your child ever had the effect of holding a mirror to your life? Whether in relation to exams, sporting achievement or other success, there have been times when I have felt proud that our children have done well simply because it has reflected well on me. To my shame, the reverse of that has been when things have not gone according to plan – when they have missed the mark in some way – and my initial concern has been to wonder what others will think of me and of my parenting.

It's probably not best to measure our personal significance by our children's achievements – or failures!

Choose your battles. If we make every issue a battle to fight not only will we wear ourselves out, but, more importantly, our children will never learn which things are really important.

I remember a psychologist saying to me, 'Some parents make a dreadful mistake: they want to be their child's best friend.' He said that while we might well reach that point later in life, we shouldn't have it as a goal when our children are young. 'Your child has got best friends in school, but parents are different,' he continued. 'They have to be prepared to say and do things that best friends are not prepared to say and do. Parents have to say no sometimes.' He's right. As parents, we have to say difficult things at times. We have to be willing to take hits in the popularity stakes. And we can't expect our kids to understand some of the decisions we believe we have to make.

I think of a young girl sleeping rough who said, 'I used to moan that my parents wanted me in at a certain time every night. I wish somebody cared what time I came home now.'

If we listen to our
children when they
are five, six and seven,
there's just a chance
they'll listen to us when
they are 15, 16, and 17.

Values are more often caught than taught.
We so often worry with our children that
'Nothing is going in!' but the problem can
be the opposite: not a word is lost. What we
say and do has a profound effect upon their
lives, forever.

When my children were small we would often say the same little prayer before they went to sleep. Quite recently, my daughter became seriously ill. Late one night, just after she'd had a major operation, her husband and I were standing at her bedside in the high dependency unit of the hospital. As we were about to leave she said, 'Would you say a little prayer, Dad?' The three of us held hands and I said the childhood prayer again. And suddenly the old tradition came down the decades and brought comfort as we reached out to arms stronger than our own.

Lord, keep us safe this night,
Secure from all our fears.
May angels guard us whilst we sleep,
Till morning light appears.
Amen.

PRAISE DOES WONDERS FOR THE SENSE OF HEARING.

ONE MUM SAID: 'EVERY
TIME I HEAR AN EXPERT
GIVE A "FOOLPROOF"
WAY TO DEAL WITH THE
KIDS, I FIND THAT MINE
ARE AN EXCEPTION TO
THE RULE!'

One parent said: 'As parents we can easily catch ourselves thinking, 'What am I doing wrong?' Then, through a timely conversation, we discover that we're not doing anything wrong – that's just the way it is. Looking at other people's situations can help us take a fresh look at our own. A friend of mine has five children – all completely different. To me, she's a kind of supermum. But through talking to her, I realise that she has the same worries and concerns as me and, as a result, I feel affirmed as a single parent that what I'm doing is actually OK.'

If your children are small, cup their head in your hands and look into their eyes when they're trying to tell you something that is really important to them.

BE THE FIRST TO
SAY SORRY.

My daughter's bedroom was always immaculate: books were arranged in alphabetical order, socks were colour-coded, and soft toys gathered together in friendship groups. On the other hand, my son's bedroom was not tidy. In fact it was a dangerous place to enter without having had several inoculations. I have seen cockroaches striding out of that bedroom carrying suitcases and complaining, 'We're sorry, but we're just not prepared to live in there any longer!'

I remember once deciding to glance under the bed. A wondrous sight greeted my eyes: old apples, browned and decaying, old crisp packets, browned and decaying, and old underpants … well, I'm sure you get the idea.

But perhaps we ought not to get too uptight about it. A mother wrote to me some time ago; her son had just left for university. She said, 'Suddenly I walked past a too tidy bedroom.'

An unsustainable pace of life can creep up on us unawares. Take a stock check and ask yourself if you can keep going with your rhythm of life. If necessary, take drastic action to change things. Your children may not be at every club and activity, but you – and they – will have time to breathe.

RULES WITHOUT RELATIONSHIP LEAD TO REBELLION.

ELIOT. AGE 18.

Spot your child's potential. They may not fit into society's definition of success. They may not be great sports people and they may not be gifted academically, but each child is unique and has gifts to offer the world. Identify them and encourage them.

ALWAYS TAKE A SECOND LOOK.

A dad said to me recently, 'My 17-year-old's got three 'A's at A level and my 16-year-old got 10 'A stars' at GCSE. But we are worried about the 13-year-old. He's not academic at all.'

'What does he love doing?' I asked.

'Cooking,' the father answered.

'Then why not help him be the best cook he can be,' I said. 'He might leave school at 16, but perhaps by the time he's 21 he'll be a chef earning a living – playing to his strengths, doing what he does best.'

Help your children discover their strengths.

THERE'S NO ONE WAY
TO BE A PERFECT
PARENT – BUT THERE
ARE A HUNDRED WAYS
TO BE A GREAT PARENT.

WHAT A RELIEF TO
DISCOVER THAT
TANTRUMS, WHINING
AND FOOT STAMPING
WERE NORMAL – AND
THAT WAS JUST THE
MOTHERS!

I remember when my daughter was small and I would be reading her a bedtime story when the phone would ring. She would say, 'Please leave it, Dad', but I'd take the stairs two at a time and shout, 'I'll be back in a moment.' And then, after an hour, I'd remember I'd not finished the story, and I would rush back upstairs. And the light would still be on, and the book would be by her head on the pillow, but little eyes had fought to stay awake as long as they could.

Since then I've had thousands of business phone calls and almost all have been urgent. But I can't remember one that couldn't have waited ten minutes while I finished a bedtime story.

Don't relegate the humble table to some past 'golden age of the family' — there never was such a time. The fact is that whether it's eating together, working together, or playing together, the table can be a focal point in our family life.

THE REALLY REALLY BUSY PERSON'S...

NO ONE WAS EVER HEARD TO SAY ON THEIR DEATHBED: 'I WISH I HAD SPENT MORE TIME AT THE OFFICE.'

Let's consider the 18 years of childhood. Imagine that an egg-timer contains not sand, but days. When your child was born the egg-timer had in it 6,570 days. If your child is ten years old, 3,650 have already gone. You have 2,920 left. No amount of money, power or prestige can increase that number. So far as is possible, try not to miss one of them.

We recently made a significant journey down the M4. The car was packed to the gunnels with the contents of IKEA, items which we had been led to believe were essential kit for any young person starting university. Our youngest son (and the contents of the car) duly deposited at his hall of residence, we made a quieter and less cramped journey home. We reflected that not only was this day a milestone for our son, but it also marked the beginning of a brand new season for us.

We were now officially 'empty nesters' – a badge we will wear with a mixture of anticipation and pride. The time and energy required to parent four children that occupied much of our waking (and sleeping!) hours over the last 26 years has seemingly disappeared overnight, and we need to learn a new way of living. We have discovered some immediate advantages: my husband has socks in his sock drawer, bottles of nail varnish no longer adorn the coffee table, the kitchen looks the same in the morning as it did when we went to bed the night before, there is enough hot water for showers and even petrol in the car.

The time when they are children goes by so quickly! Someone once said: 'The days are long, but the years are short.'

THE REALLY REALLY BUSY PERSON'S…

Remember that bedroom strewn with crisp packets, scrunched up homework, muddy sports kit, damp towels, odd socks (and shoes!) and enough dirty underwear to start an epidemic? Of course you do. You have yelled for it to be tidied, bribed for it to be tidied, and prayed for it to be tidied. Well, one day it will be tidy. Too tidy!

You'll be free! No more birthday cakes to make in the shape of cartoon characters, no more nativity costumes to conjure up using old curtains and a tea towel, and no more solemn goldfish burials in the garden. You'll

have time to yourself. No buggies to manoeuvre into overcrowded shops, no haircuts with a wriggling toddler on your knee, no four-year-olds wandering half asleep into your bedroom, no leaving a drink for Father Christmas, no knotted hair after swimming, no trying to skip pages reading a bedtime story and getting found out.

Honey sandwiches, hide and seek, stories under the sheets, tonsils, school runs, shoe laces, lunch boxes, croup, milk teeth, cut knees, first periods and maths periods – all gone. Bringing up young children will be all done and dusted.

One day you'll say, 'It's time you kids grew up!'

And they will.

It has been well said that, 'The best thing a father can do for his children is to love their mother' and of course that works for loving fathers as well. There are obviously other reasons for investing in our couple relationship – but the fact that it benefits our children is not a bad place to start.

LAY
DOWN
THE
GUILT.

As parents, our every instinct is often to keep our children 'safe'. But if we allow that to govern our approach to parenting, always saying 'No' to any exploit that has any element of risk attached, we will be denying them the chance to develop some essential life skills.

I remember my son telling me he would never marry anybody else except me, and both my kids telling me when they were young that they would never leave home. And I remember, when they were teenagers, worrying in case they meant it.

You never stop being a parent. When they've grown up and left home, you have no authority over them at all and you can't do anything about it when they make mistakes. You just have to let them go; but when they leave, part of you goes with them.

The idea that you can have it all and do it all is an illusion. Supermum or Superdad is not out there. You can wear your underwear outside your trousers, but you still can't fly.

There is no greater gift we can give
our children than for them to grow up
knowing that regardless of their looks, their
successes or their failures, they are loved
unconditionally.

One night, when my son was very small, I was saying prayers with him. The next day I was due to go to a very important meeting, and I was more than a little nervous. I have prayed many prayers for him but on this occasion I asked him to utter one for me. This is what he said:

Dear Lord,

Please help my dad to be brave, and not to make too many mistakes.

Amen.

It's not a bad prayer for every parent.

THE REALLY REALLY BUSY PERSON'S...

Muddy
Pearl